The Nicaragua Grand Canal

Praise for the book

'*The Nicaragua Grand Canal* is a clear, balanced and accessible analysis of the background to the canal and its implications.'

Jenny Pearce, Professor Latin American Politics,
Peace Studies, University of Bradford

'This book is fluent and supple in its expression and admirably open-minded in assessing the complex challenges faced by all parties. Well done indeed!'

James Dunkerley, Professor of Latin American Politics,
Queen Mary College, University of London

'This latest briefing from LAB should become indispensable reading for anyone concerned with Nicaragua's future. It is succinct and highly readable, yet well-grounded in the wide literature on this controversial project. Beginning with the history of Nicaragua's perennial dream of a transoceanic canal, it succinctly explores its complex modern economic, political, social, and environmental implications. With convincing authority it conveys an acute sense of the hopes and uncertainties besetting the enterprise, enmeshed as it is within a dual context of international instability and the conflictive politics of Nicaragua under its second Sandinista government.'

Jane Freeland, Centre for Transnational Studies,
University of Southampton

The Nicaragua Grand Canal

Economic Miracle or *Folie de Grandeur*?

Russell White

PRACTICAL ACTION
Publishing

Practical Action Publishing Ltd
The Schumacher Centre,
Bourton on Dunsmore, Rugby,
Warwickshire, CV23 9QZ, UK
www.practicalactionpublishing.org

A catalogue record for this book is available from the British Library.
A catalogue record for this book has been requested from the Library of Congress.

ISBN 9781853394091 Hardback
ISBN 9781909014107 Paperback
ISBN 9781909014121 Library Ebook
ISBN 9781909014114 Ebook

Citation: White, R., (2015) *The Nicaragua Grand Canal – Economic Miracle or Folie de Grandeur?*, Rugby, UK: Practical Action Publishing, <http://dx.doi.org/10.3362/9781909014121>

Since 1974, Practical Action Publishing has published and disseminated books and information in support of international development work throughout the world. Practical Action Publishing is a trading name of Practical Action Publishing Ltd (Company Reg. No. 1159018), the wholly owned publishing company of Practical Action. Practical Action Publishing trades only in support of its parent charity objectives and any profits are covenanted back to Practical Action (Charity Reg. No. 247257, Group VAT Registration No. 880 9924 76).

Cover design by Andrew Corbett
Cover image: Bigstock
Typeset by Allzone Digital Services Ltd.
Printed in the United Kingdom

Contents

http://dx.doi.org/10.3362/9781909014121.000

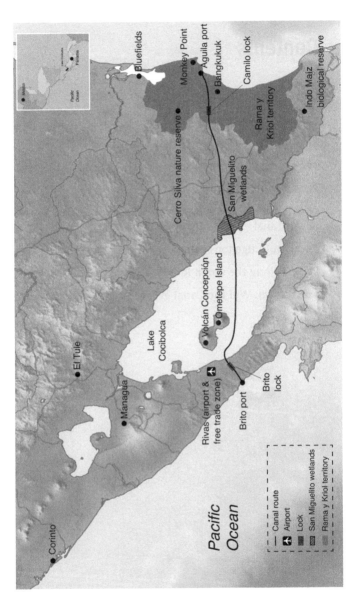

Pacific Ocean

Corinto

Managua

El Tule

Lake Cocibolca

Volcán Concepción
Ometepe Island

Rivas (airport & free trade zone)

Brito port

Brito lock

Cerro Silva nature reserve

San Miguelito wetlands

Bluefields

Monkey Point

Aguila port

Bangkukuk

Camilo lock

Rama y Kriol territory

Indo Maíz biological reserve

Mexico
Pacific Ocean
Panama

Canal route
Airport
Lock
San Miguelito wetlands
Rama y Kriol territory

Introduction

Every schoolchild can name the world's two most famous canals: the Suez and the Panama. Soon, there may be a third: the Nicaragua Grand Interoceanic Canal, intended to complement and eventually replace the Panama Canal and provide a modern link for shipping between the Atlantic and the Pacific oceans. However they are financed, such vast projects invariably project the trading and imperial ambitions of the great powers – France and Britain in the case of Suez, and France and the United States for Panama. The Nicaraguan Canal appears to be a project for the new kid on the block – China.

The Nicaragua Canal broke ground on Monday 22 December 2014 at a ceremony at Tola Rivas near the tiny fishing village of Brito on the Pacific Coast. Both Nicaraguan President, Daniel Ortega, and Wang Jing, the billionaire businessman behind Chinese construction company Hong Kong Nicaragua Canal Development Group (HKND), spoke at the ceremony. Ortega heralded the project as a boon for both Nicaragua and Latin America, noting that 'Today we are a region where we defend the principle of sovereignty, where we hold up the region as a region of peace, and therefore it is not an accident that this project is being carried out when, in our Americas, we have succeeded in making this great historic leap towards integration and unity of all our peoples' (Small, 2015). Ortega also said that the Chinese 'have not come to Nicaragua with occupying troops' but have instead 'come to share their resources, their capabilities, their development, their technology, their science . . . with

http://dx.doi.org/10.3362/9781909014121.001

the Nicaraguan people'. The Canal project, he said, represented the 'meeting of two peoples, the glorious people of China with the glorious Nicaraguan people' (Small, 2015).

HKND's website, meanwhile, carried an excerpt from Wang's speech, which was similarly ebullient in its attempt to capture the historical significance of the Canal: 'With roar of the truck traversing time and space, the century-old dream has become a reality. It carries Nicaraguans' happiness and bright future, embodies our painstaking efforts and will change the status of maritime trade' (HKND, 2014b). Wang also referred to the challenges that the Canal project presented, but assured the audience that HKND, working with the Nicaraguan Government and 'world-class companies and scientists' from 'the US, UK, Belgium, Australia and China', would be able to overcome them (HKND, 2014b). Although the ceremony itself was accompanied by some fanfare, it was actually largely symbolic, marking little more than the start of construction of access roads needed to transport large scale machinery, rather than the building of the Canal itself. Moreover, in the months since the groundbreaking ceremony, no construction activity has actually taken place.

On 14 June 2013 the Nicaraguan Congress, at the instigation of President Daniel Ortega, passed Law 840, the *Ley especial para el desarrollo de infraestructura y transporte nicaragüense atingente al Canal, zona de libre comercio e infraestructuras asociadas*. This law granted the HKND a 100-year concession (an initial 50 years, with an option to renew for a further 50) to build an interoceanic canal through Nicaragua. The concession was agreed with quite startling speed. It was passed in a mere seven days, and it was passed without consultation with affected stakeholders and before any detailed studies had been undertaken into the Canal's construction feasibility, economic viability, and likely social, economic and environmental impact.

At 172 miles (278km), the proposed Canal will be significantly longer than the Panama Canal which stretches for 51 miles (77km). Intended to run from the mouth of the Río Brito on the Pacific Coast through Lake Cocibolca (also known as Lake Nicaragua) to the mouth of the Punta Gorda River on the Caribbean seaboard, this will be the world's largest construction project. Alongside the Canal itself, the project will see the construction of two new deep-water sea ports (Brito Port on the Pacific Coast and Águila Port on the Caribbean Coast), tourist complexes (including one at Ometepe Island in Lake Nicaragua), an airport (at Rivas) and satellite towns along the Canal's path as well as the establishment of a Free Trade Zone (again at Rivas). Construction of these facilities will commence when the building of the canal is further advanced. The Canal will also see improvements made to the ports at Corinto and Bluefields. New highways (totaling some 595.66 km) and a new railroad will also be built, together with two bridges (Oquist, 2015: 14).

While the project has been well received among many Nicaraguans, for whom the prospect of a Nicaraguan canal has been a cherished ambition, it has upset many of the communities that live along the proposed route. Serious concerns have been raised by environmental groups, farmers, and indigenous communities about the viability and desirability of the Canal. Outside Nicaragua, the Canal has attracted a degree of scepticism and scorn.

Political opponents of Ortega, among whom are many former Sandinista allies, argue that the Canal project represents the ultimate vanity project, a *folie de grandeur* that speaks to the cult of personality that surrounds the President or is ostensibly a front which is designed to mask Ortega's manoeuverings ahead of the 2016 election. Noted Uruguayan author Eduardo Galeano accused Ortega of selling 'Nicaragua to a Chinese businessman' and of falling for a 'dubious Chinese yarn' (Alpieldelapalabra, 2014). On the day that the project broke ground, Sergio Ramírez, Ortega's former Vice-President turned staunch critic of the administration, tweeted 'Today is a tragic day for Nicaragua. With the Chinese Canal, its sovereignty is once again surrendered to a foreign power' (Anderson, 2015).

Environmental groups within and without Nicaragua, meanwhile, argue that the government is playing fast and loose with Nicaragua's patrimony. Environmentalists are concerned that the law granting HKND the concession includes a section suggesting that current environmental laws should be amended. This suggests a government willing to ride roughshod over the environment. As Belgian born ecologist and entomologist Jean-Michel Maes wrote in *Revista Envío*, 'the [Canal] law gives the impression of being more concerned with economic development than the nation's natural heritage' (Maes, 2014). Environmentalists are particularly concerned that the route chosen for the Canal will pass through Lake Cocibolca, the largest source of fresh water in Central America. Indeed, reports indicate that some 55 miles (106.8km) of the Canal's length will be through the lake (Zuidema, 2015). Environmentalists worry that dredging the lake and removing sediment (necessary because the lake has an average depth of between nine and fifteen metres depending on the source consulted) will have a serious effect on water quality, and will potentially render water from the lake undrinkable.

The Ortega administration and HKND argue that the economic benefits of the Canal to the country will be enormous – though this does not seem to be borne out by the figures that have been cited in various sources. Under the terms of the agreement, HKND will pay the Nicaraguan Government a fee of US$10 m per year for 10 years. After that initial ten-year period has expired, the Nicaraguan Government will receive a percentage of canal revenues starting at 1 per cent and increasing year on year (Lee, 2014). HKND have suggested that the Canal's construction will generate 50,000 jobs with a further 200,000 jobs being created once the Canal comes into operation. According to Canal spokesperson Telémaco Talavera, the free trade zone that is being built as part of the wider canal project will itself employ some 113,000 people working in businesses that have interests in manufacturing, logistics and shipping (Johnson, 2015). Actual operation of the canal will generate 3,700 jobs by 2020, increasing to 12,700 jobs by 2050, while the projected tourist complexes will account for a further 3,000 jobs (Oquist, 2015: 33). The government anticipates that the Canal will effectively double Nicaragua's Gross Domestic Product and thus enable it to fulfil its stated goal of eradicating extreme poverty. As government minister Paul Oquist noted 'We need a way out of poverty, the Canal will provide this' (Nicaragua Solidarity Campaign, 2014). Nicaragua is the second poorest country in the Western Hemisphere after Haiti and while the last few years have seen GDP grow, exports double, single-digit inflation, increased investment from foreign companies and declining levels of inequality, extreme poverty continues to be a problem. The Economic Commission for Latin America and the Caribbean (ECLAC) reported that 74 per cent of Nicaraguans live in 'multidimensional poverty' (multidimensional poverty indices cover health, education, poor living standards, income, disempowerment, and the threat of violence). That compares to 28 per cent for Latin America in general (Kinzer, 2015). The economy is currently growing at 4 per cent. The Nicaraguan Government believes that for extreme poverty to be eradicated it needs to grow at 8 per cent.

History of the Canal

The idea of a Canal through Nicaragua is very long-standing and is, as a Borges & Asociados report noted, 'a foundation narrative of Nicaraguan national identity' (Nicaragua News Bulletin, 2014). It was floated by Hernán Cortés, the conquistador of Mexico, by *El Libertador* Simón Bolívar, as well as by future French President Louis-Napoleon Bonaparte, who proposed it in a detailed pamphlet, written in 1846 while he was in prison. Although many people had considered what a Canal across Nicaragua could offer, and some basic surveys were conducted, no concerted plan to actually build the Canal was made until the nineteenth century.

'The Nicaragua Canal', wrote historian Lawrence Clayton, was 'one of the great American dreams of the nineteenth century' (Clayton, 1987: 323). Clayton went on to observe that it was the lure of the Canal that drew the US to Central America in the first place. Many American commentators were enthused by the trade possibilities that a Canal through the Isthmus would provide. The government of John Quincy Adams undertook negotiations with the Nicaraguan Government in 1825. Twenty-four years later, in 1849, the American industrialist Cornelius Vanderbilt secured a concession from Nicaragua to build the Canal and a year later he established the American Atlantic and Pacific Ship Canal Company. Nicaragua's suitability as the location for the Canal was established by a survey undertaken by Colonel Orville W. Childs at Vanderbilt's behest (Clayton, 1987: 326).

American enthusiasm for the Canal would extend beyond mid-century. Writing in *The North American Review* in 1881, former US President Ulysses S. Grant noted that the Canal 'would increase our commercial facilities beyond calculation' (Grant, 1881: 109). As a soldier, Grant had had a most unpleasant experience crossing Panama with the 4th US Infantry Regiment. One hundred men had lost their lives en route, mainly succumbing to cholera. It was this experience that roused his interest in building a Canal. As President, Grant, like Vanderbilt, had sent engineering expeditions to Central America during the 1870s to determine the best route for the Canal. The Ammen Commission endorsed Nicaragua as the best site for the Canal in 1876, just as Childs had done. Not only was Nicaragua considerably closer to the United States than Panama, the other leading option, it would also present fewer engineering challenges and thus would cost less.

The Maritime Canal Company was contracted with the Nicaraguan Government to build the Canal in 1887, but the economic crisis of 1893 caused the project to collapse (Clayton, 1987: 328). The 1898 war with Spain once again stimulated the interest of the American public in a Canal across the Isthmus. While Nicaragua had consistently been endorsed as the best location for the Canal, history would unfold differently.

Clayton notes that by 1901, debate about where to build a Canal had turned into a 'battle' between Nicaragua and Panama. The Inter-Oceanic Canal Commission led by Admiral Walker, which had been expected to support Nicaragua, plumped instead for Panama. The catalyst for that judgement had been the decision of the French New Panama Canal Company led by Philippe Bunau-Varilla to slash the price of the various surveys, maps and drawings pertaining to a Canal in Panama together with the related equipment and the Panama railroad itself. In addition, William Nelson Cromwell, who had been hired by Bunau-Varilla to lobby Congress, planted a story in *The New York Sun* that the Momotombo volcano, situated on the shores of Lake Managua, had erupted. Famously, he followed this up by ensuring that every senator received a leaflet three days before the final vote on the route of the Canal, which included a picture of a one cent Nicaraguan stamp depicting Momotombo.

The eruption of Mount Pelée on Martinique on 8 May 1902, which caused 30,000 deaths, was the final nail in the coffin for the Nicaraguan Canal. Momotombo itself erupted on 14 May 1902. On 19 June, the US Senate voted 42 to 34 for the Panamanian option (Clayton, 1987: 351–352). Clayton writes that 'Nicaragua lost the opportunity of the century to become the crossroads of the world. The boom that befell Panama bypassed Nicaragua' (Clayton, 1987: 352).

Nicaragua's national icon Augusto César Sandino later returned to the theme of the Canal in his 'Plan de realización del supremo sueño de Bolívar' (Sandino, 1929); a document that outlines a 44-point plan to establish Latin American unity. Sandino conceived of the Canal as a fundamentally Latin American undertaking rather than a project to be carried out by a corporation or a country from outside the region. Sandino was keen that the countries of Latin America not 'transfer, sell, surrender or rent' the Canal, since to do so would 'compromise the stability of Latin American sovereignty and independence' (Sandino, 1929: 36). The idea of a Nicaraguan Canal built by Latin Americans was part of a wider call for an alliance between Latin American nations – 'indispensable', according to Sandino, 'to maintain unscathed this independence in the face of the imperialist pretensions of the United States of North America' (Sandino, 1929: 31). The Canal is referred to in a number of the 44 *puntos básicos* that Sandino outlines and sits alongside other calls to declare the abolition of the Monroe

Doctrine, establish a single Latin American nationality, a Latin American army, and a Latin American court of justice (Sandino, 1929: 31–39).

Sandino had taken particular umbrage at the Bryan-Chamorro Treaty which General Emiliano Chamorro, then Nicaraguan minister to the United States, had negotiated with US Secretary of State William Jennings Bryan and which was signed on 5 August 1914. In a piece on the Canal for the anti-Sandinista magazine *Confidencial*, Octavio Enríquez writes that 'On more than one occasion, various generations of Nicaraguans have described the Chamorro Bryan treaty [. . .] as the worst agreement in the history of the country' (Enríquez, 2014). It was Sandino who coined the term 'vendepatria' - 'seller of the homeland', a phrase that has adorned banners at some of the protests that have taken place against the canal. The Bryan-Chamorro treaty, which Sandino saw as a betrayal of the nation, granted the US the exclusive right to build a Nicaragua Canal. In effect, it stymied any Nicaraguan or non-US attempt to resurrect a canal project within Nicaragua. Ten days after the treaty's signing, the Panama Canal opened for business and the Nicaragua Canal was never built. That treaty was only, in fact, revoked in 1970.

Sandino's vision of the Canal was picked up by the *Frente Sandinista de Liberación Nacional*'s (FSLN's) chief theoretician Carlos Fonseca, who inserted the story of the Canal into a wider narrative about imperialism's impact on Nicaraguan history in two texts: *Nicaragua: Hora Cero* (1969) and *Viva Sandino* (1974). For Fonseca, the geopolitical potential for a Canal rendered Nicaragua susceptible to 'violent episodes'. Political scientist Luciano Baracco writes that the Canal 'acted like a magnet to the pretensions of the major imperialist powers of the nineteenth and twentieth centuries' (Baracco, 2005: 72). Baracco observes that Fonseca was keen to show the emergence of the FSLN as a 'logical outcome of, and the necessary solution to, "more than four centuries of foreign aggression and oppression"' (Baracco, 2005: 68).

Fonseca's history charts numerous US interventions in Nicaragua's affairs, starting with the Monroe Doctrine, enunciated by President James Monroe in his State of the Union address to Congress in 1823. It moves on to the Clayton-Bulwer Treaty of 1850, which sought to reduce tensions between Britain and the US over a proposed canal across the Isthmus; the US Navy's destruction of San Juan del Norte in 1854; the country's takeover by the American *filibustero* William Walker who ruled as President from 1856–57; US agent Lewis Hanke's attempt to intervene on behalf of Nicaragua's Conservatives following the Liberal Party's rise to power in 1893; the removal of nationalist president José Santos Zelaya in 1909; the intervention by American gun boats on behalf of the Conservatives in 1910; the killing of the lawyer and politician Benjamín Zeledón in 1912 by US marines at the battle of Coyetepe Hill; the Bryan-Chamorro Treaty signed in 1914; and the US occupation of the country which lasted from 1912 until 1933 with a break of only one year (Fonseca, 1969).

The occupation, of course, was resisted by Augusto Sandino until his death in 1934 at the hands of National Guardsmen under the command of Anastasio Somoza García. The subsequent establishment of the US-supported Somoza dictatorship was thus the latest in a long line of unwelcome interventions from foreign powers, particularly the United States (Baracco, 2005: 68). For Fonseca, Nicaragua had been a 'victim for more than a century of Yankee aggression' (Fonseca, 1969). With the rise to power of Somoza, Nicaragua became, in the words of Fonseca, a 'base' for the said 'Yankee aggression' with Somoza a stooge for American imperialist foreign policy within the region (Fonseca, 1969).

One can only imagine what Fonseca and Sandino would make of the concession granted HKND by Ortega. Reports indicate that at some of the rallies that have taken place to protest against the Canal, Wang Jing, has been portrayed as a latter-day version of William Walker (Watts, 2015), a foreigner who is seeking to take over the country. Enríquez suggests that Ortega has redefined the concept of sovereignty as 'the possibility of having some resources, [and] a regular income, which would make Nicaragua no longer as dependent as it is today' (Enríquez, 2014).

Of course, it would be impossible for the Canal to be built today without funding from outside the region. Moreover, the fact that the Canal project as it stands now is at odds with Sandino's original vision matters not to Ortega nor, as opinion polls demonstrate, to the majority of the Nicaraguan people. A posting on the Nicaragua News Network from November 2014, referred to data from polling agencies M & R and Borge & Asociados, indicating that about three-quarters of Nicaraguans thought that Ortega was doing a good or a very good job (Nicaragua News Bulletin, 2014). Ortega has sought to present himself as the heir to Sandino's legacy, the man who can realize Sandino's vision and fulfil Nicaragua's destiny. It is not just Sandino's legacy that is being invoked here. Ortega has looked to insert himself into a tradition of pan-Latin American thinking that incorporates iconic figures such as Bolívar and José Martí, whom Carlos Fonseca called 'the Apostle' (Fonseca, 1974: 32).

The Canal and Sandinista Tensions

The Nicaraguan Canal has highlighted long-standing tensions between Ortega and former allies-turned-opponents, including: Sergio Ramírez; Ernesto Cardenal, the liberation theologian and former Sandinista Culture Minister; Dora María Téllez, former Minister of Health, who, as Comandante 2, was a key military leader of the Sandinista insurrection, and Carlos Fernando Chamorro, the one-time editor of the Sandinista newspaper *Barricada*, who now runs *Confidencial* magazine, amongst other journalistic ventures. Significantly, all of these figures retain considerable influence internationally, something demonstrated through their prominence in western media reports criticizing Ortega, HKND and the Canal project.

They accuse Ortega of using the Canal project to perpetuate his presidency. The Canal concession, they argue, is typical of a President who is overly concerned with his own image and constructing a legacy. As Ramírez told Jon Lee Anderson: 'Ortega wants to make it appear that his tenure in power is indispensable in order to consummate this long-term project' (Anderson, 2014). Ramírez, like other former Sandinistas, has long been a critic of Ortega's thirst for power. 'Ortega and his followers don't believe in democracy', he told British journalist Nick Caistor. 'They see it as something that is not necessary. What they want is to stay in power at all costs', he continued (Caistor, 2009). For figures such as Ramírez, then, the Canal project is really the latest and the most ambitious chapter in a wider story, one that in 2009 saw Nicaragua's Supreme

Court alter the constitution so that Ortega could stand for re-election.

Critics see this as the rise of 'Danielismo', and point to the 'cult of personality' that surrounds Ortega. Some argue that such is the degree of personalism (and attendant problems of nepotism and corruption) at the heart of the administration, that the Ortega family now resembles the Somoza family dynasty that ruled Nicaragua for over 42 years (1936–79), and which the FSLN fought so hard to remove. Some commentators, for example, claim that Ortega owns much of Nicaragua's free trade infrastructure (Arsenault, 2011). Writing in *Time*, Tim Rogers notes that the way in which Ortega and other Sandinistas have used aid – particularly large-scale aid from Venezuela – to purchase Nicaraguan companies and 'corner entire industries in Nicaragua' is 'startlingly reminiscent of the personal fiefdom [the Somozas] made of Nicaragua during their long rule' (Rogers, 2011). While the government is very keen to stress 'Ortega's fealty to Sandino', and Ortega continues to use the language of anti-imperialism to rail against the forces of global capitalism, many commentators argue that 'Ortega is a Sandinista in name only' (Kinzner, 2015). For Stephen Kinzer, Ortega is 'turning into just the kind of pro-business autocrat he spent years of his life fighting' (Kinzer, 2015).

Such comments are indicative of the ongoing struggle for the 'soul' of *Sandinismo*. The Sandinista Renovation Movement (MRS), which was founded by Ramírez in 1994, is predicated on the belief that Ortega has lost sight of the principles of *Sandinismo*. The founding of the MRS 'took', according to Thomas Walker and Christine Wade, 'most of the professional and intellectual leaders out of the FSLN' (Walker and Wade, 2011: 68). Detractors point to Ortega's fostering of links with former enemies from within the business elite in the form of the Superior Council of Private Enterprise, the right-wing *Partido Liberal Constitucionalista* (PLC) led by Arnoldo Alemán, and conservative sections of the Catholic Church led by Cardinal Miguel Obando y Bravo. Relations with big business, foreign investors, and wealthier sections of Nicaraguan society have been fostered through tax laws (the 2012 Tax Concertation Law for instance) granting or extending concessions to the wealthy. When Obando y Bravo officiated at the marriage of Ortega and Rosario Murillo just before Ortega's re-election in 2006, it signalled a rapprochement between the Sandinista couple and a key counter-revolutionary figure of the 1980s. Ortega's engagement with the business elite and the Catholic Church is consistent with the politics of pragmatism he practices. It is this politics that led Tim Rogers to characterize Ortega as 'as a masterful political operator – a pragmatist who believes in power' and an 'opportunist rather than an ideologue' (Rogers cited in Arsenault, 2011).

The Economics of the Canal

At the moment no one outside of the government or HKND can quite work out how the Canal project is going to be financed or whether it is actually even needed. Some have questioned whether there will be enough shipping volume over the next few decades to really justify or sustain a second canal within the Americas. There is competition, not only from the recently expanded Panama Canal, but from the alternative route to the US Atlantic Coast via Suez and from the potential opening of a northern passage, made possible by the retreat of Arctic ice. Suez has recently had a US$8 bn refit, opened by the Sisi government with great patriotic fervour, to ready it for more and larger vessels. Tellingly, Shadi Hamid, a senior fellow at the Brookings Institution said of Egypt's role: 'It's not even really about economics. It's about national pride' (Malsin, 2015).

The economic issue turns on three constraints on shipping imposed by the existing Panama Canal: limits on overall capacity (the number of ships that can transit); limits on the availability of water to fill it; and limits on the size of ships that can be accommodated by the width and depth of the Canal and its locks.

Why the need for a new Canal?

On capacity, David Taylor, Panama representative for the Institution of Civil Engineers, told the *International Business Times*: 'The demand to ship things from Asia to the East Coast is there, and it's a big demand, but it's not vast. [. . .] We don't have hundreds of ships queuing up waiting to go through the Panama Canal' (Lee, 2014).

Others differ. A recent article in the *Miami Herald* quotes Rodolfo Sabonge, a former Vice President of the Panama Canal Authority, who said the main impetus for expansion was that the Canal was reaching capacity, rather than just the need to handle big ships. The 2007 global financial crisis had at best 'bought some time', as trade levels dropped. The recent expansion of the Canal 'has come just in time', he said. 'The canal wasn't going to be able to handle the number of ships' (Whitefield, 2015).

HKND, of course, has its own vision, but studiously avoids making direct comparisons with Panama. The company's website points to three main 'trends' which, it says, supports the building of a canal in Nicaragua: the growth of maritime trade, globalization, and shifting global trade patterns. Even with the slowdown in trade growth following the 2008 economic crisis, the increase in orders for very large container ships together with the growth of markets in the Economic South mean that a second canal is necessary. The company believes that trade between Asia and the Americas will continue to grow – and indeed the company estimates the value of goods passing through the Panama and Nicaraguan Canals by 2030 at some US$1.4 tn. During a talk on the Canal at London's Canning House, government minister Paul Oquist stated that, once completed, some 900 million tons will move through the Canal each year. 'The Grand Canal', he said, 'will assume 5 per cent of world trade transport' (Oquist, 2015: 28).

Another concern is that the Panama Canal will not be able to accommodate the growing trend towards ever larger container ships. The Nicaragua Canal is designed to accommodate the largest ships, including the Triple-E ships of the Norwegian Maersk Line. These ships are 400 m long, 59 m wide, 73 m high, 12.6 m deep, and can hold up to 23,000 containers. According to Oquist, they consume 35 per cent less fuel per container than vessels that can only take 13,000 containers (Oquist, 2015: 27) and are thus potentially much cheaper to operate. These leviathans will never be able to traverse the Panama Canal. Some doubts remain, however, about the speed with which these largest ships will be adopted and the routes on which they will be deployed, with limitations imposed not only by canals, but size restrictions at ports.

The aim of the $5 bn refit of the Panama Canal, now almost complete and due to be officially opened in 2016, is aimed at increasing overall capacity, economizing on water use and accommodating somewhat larger ships. A 2009 article in *The Economist* magazine noted that whilst in 2000 it was the case that the Panama Canal was wide and deep enough to accommodate some 85 per cent of the world's container fleet, by 2007 that figure had dropped to 57 per cent and by 2011 it predicted that it would be less than half (*The Economist*, 2009). According to Oquist, post-Panamax vessels will account for 30 per cent of the container ships traversing the oceans and will carry 60–70 per cent of world trade (Oquist, 2015: 29). Even after the refit, however, the Panama Canal will still only be able to accommodate ships that hold 13,000 containers. Triple-E ships will be confined to other routes, until the Nicaragua Canal is completed.

The greatest uncertainty, however, concerns water. Canals with locks require a supply of water from rivers, lakes or aqueducts to fill the locks and every transit requires an expenditure of water or an expenditure of energy to pump the water back up to a reservoir. The Panama Canal refit aims to reduce its water requirements by recycling some of the water, but the cumulative effects of deforestation and climate change pose serious questions about the Canal's long term viability (Hamilton, 2008).

Cost and funding

Estimates suggest that the Nicaragua Canal is going to cost between $40 bn and $50 bn to build, an enormous sum for a country whose entire GDP stood at $11.26 bn in 2013. Yet the source of such funding remains a mystery. Moreover, the fact that HKND has been unwilling or unable to outline precisely how the Canal is going to be paid for has not done anything for the credibility of the project. Doubts remain that such an amount can actually be raised, particularly without the release of economic and environmental feasibility and impact studies. Some news reports claim that only $200 m of funding has thus far been sourced, just 0.5 per cent of the minimum amount required. Wang Jing told the BBC's China editor Carrie Gracie that 'I cannot let this project become an international joke' (Gracie, 2015), yet this is what Wang is risking.

Telémaco Talavera had stated previously that details of the project's financing would be provided before it broke ground on 22 December 2014. While the project did indeed get under way three days before Christmas with the building of access roads at the mouth of the Brito River, the promised report which the government had commissioned from American management consultants McKinsey & Co was not forthcoming. Paul Oquist said that the report had been delayed because amendments needed to be made following changes to the route of the Canal. Nevertheless, as each month passes with no sign of a published report, scepticism within and without Nicaragua is building.

HKND officials have consistently claimed that funding is in place but that the detail remains confidential. At a public meeting in Managua in July 2014, public relations manager Dong Lu told the audience that 'These affairs are secret because the companies are trading on the stock exchange and there are details that it is not proper to reveal' (Lu cited in *Revista Envío*, 2014). Wang assured *The Daily Telegraph* in an interview published in July 2014 that his company had investors lined up from both China and a host of other countries. Wang's confidence is clearly shared by the government. The President of the Nicaraguan Canal Authority Manuel Coronel Kautz anticipates that a stock listing will be made once some issues over land titles are resolved. According to Coronel, once that listing takes place, 'Four, five, or 10 Chinese companies will buy up the shares and it'll all be done' (cited in Johnson, 2015). This confidence may well be dented by the recent (July 2015) extreme volatility of the Chinese stock exchange, growing doubts about whether the slowing Chinese economy can avoid a hard landing and the nervousness of many investors. Moreover, by not directly naming these investors, HKND and the Nicaraguan Government are damaging the project's credibility both within Nicaragua and abroad.

Those critical of the project have questioned the extent to which HKND is really serious about seeing this project through, and there have also been allegations of corruption. In a piece for *The New Yorker*, Jon Lee Anderson observed that the opacity of the negotiations has led 'many Nicaraguans [to] assume that Ortega has a private financial arrangement with Wang' (Anderson, 2014).

Wang Jing's Companies

Contributing to the uncertainty is the fact that comparatively little is known about Wang. *Forbes* magazine lists him as the twelfth richest man in China with a fortune of $6.4 bn (Global Consilium, 2015). Writing in *Confidencial*, Santiago Villa noted that Wang is the majority partner in some 21 companies. The most important of these are

Skyrizon Aircraft Holdings Ltd, Southeast Asia Agriculture Development Group Inc, Beijing Tiangjuan Culture Media Ltd, Beijing Guanwei Sports Culture Communication Ltd, Beijing Xinwei Tongxin Technology Corporation and Beijing Dayang Xinhe Investment Management. These companies span a range of interests including mining, infrastructure and telecommunications, though some see them as shell companies. Reports into Wang's background suggest that most of his fortune has come through Xinwei and through the activities of the Southeast Asia Agriculture Development Group Inc, and particularly through an investment made in a Cambodian gold mine.

The last of these companies, Beijing Dayang Xinhe Investment Management, is, according to Villa, 'the mother company of the network of 15 companies that constitute [. . .] HKND' (Villa, 2014). Villa goes on to note that none of them 'was set up with more than US$50,000 capital'. The companies are headquartered or registered in places as diverse as the Cayman Islands and the Netherlands (Villa, 2014). The fact that the various subsidiary companies that constitute HKND are based in different countries would, according to Villa, make it very difficult to pursue a lawsuit against the company. This means that, if the Canal project collapses, it will be difficult for the Nicaraguan Government to extract compensation from Wang through the courts.

Whatever his achievements, Wang has no experience of implementing an infrastructure project of this size. Moreover, Xinwei's record when it comes to investing in projects outside China is patchy. The company has secured contracts in some 20 countries, yet none of these projects is actually up and running. It has also not escaped the attention of critics that Xinwei has yet to start work on the wireless network for which it was awarded the contract in 2012 by the Nicaraguan State in a deal estimated to be worth $700 m (Smith, 2014) and for which it beat off competition from companies based in Taiwan and Hong Kong.

The role of the Chinese Government

Despite HKND's protestations that the canal is a private enterprise (a view also expressed by Costa Rican President Luis Guillermo Solís) many find it hard to believe that the Chinese Government is not in some way behind this project. Moreover, as the former Nicaraguan ambassador to the United States, Arturo Cruz, told the Reuters news agency, 'If the Canal goes ahead, it will be because the Chinese Government wants it to, and the financing will come from China's various state firms' (Stagardter, 2014). A similar point is made by Kissinger Institute director Robert Daly. The Canal, he says,

> . . . couldn't have gone forward on this scale, if it is going forward, without an OK and without a buy-in from the Chinese Government. [. . .] [T]he implications of the project, not so much financially but in terms of trade relations and power projections, and strategic relations are simply too great for the Chinese Government to let it go forward simply because there's a businessman in Hong Kong who wants to make an investment (cited in Huang and Billing, 2015).

The perspectives offered by Cruz and Daly reinforce views offered by critics of the government within Nicaragua itself. For figures such as Carlos Chamorro, the involvement of the Chinese Government would change the dynamic of the project. In a piece for *El País*, Chamorro observed that if this is a project whose viability depends entirely on the political goodwill of the People's Republic of China, the geopolitical, environmental and institutional implications will be completely different for our country. If this is the case, as the secretive tone seems to indicate, then we are facing a project that will promote the interests of Chinese power at any cost (Chamorro, 2014).

Although China's Ministry of Commerce recommended through an advert that Chinese companies should avoid getting involved in this project, there appear to be plenty of state companies that have ignored this advice (Villa, 2014). HKND's own website points to the involvement of a number of Chinese companies, amongst which are some heavy hitters, including China Railway SIYUAN Survey and Design Group, and the state-owned Changjiang Institute of Survey, Planning, Design and Research which worked on the Three Gorges project.

The Geopolitics of the Canal

According to Juan Gabriel Tokatlian 'In the same way that the Panama Canal was the US Canal in the 20th century, a Nicaragua Canal would eventually be the Chinese Canal in the 21st century' (Tokatlian cited in Háskel, 2014). The Canal project fits with China's wider strategy to extend its influence over maritime trade, and to develop trade routes that are beyond the control of western powers. This ambition was described by Chinese President Xi Jinping in 2013 as a 21st-Century 'Maritime Silk Road' running through and facilitating trade within Southeast and South Asia (Jinping, 2013). It is this that is underpinning the proposed construction of the Kra Isthmus Canal through southern Thailand, another project that is supposedly being funded through private investment, albeit with a budget of $28 bn and a projected construction time double that of the proposed Nicaragua Canal.

The development of China's maritime trade has also seen the Chinese invest significantly in port infrastructure in places such as Piraeus and Antwerp, and is driven by the growth in Chinese shipping. China has emerged as a major maritime power in recent years. Statistics from the World Bank indicate that China's container shipping is three times that of the United States. The Canal with its accompanying deep water ports on Nicaragua's Atlantic and Pacific coasts would facilitate China's trade with the United States and Mexico. The port at Brito will have a capacity of 1.95 million 20-foot containers, while that at Punto Águila will be able to take 2.65 million containers (López, 2014). Whereas at the moment much of Nicaragua's import and export trade moves through Puerto Cortés in Honduras and Puerto Limón in Costa Rica, this will change with the building of the deep water Brito and Águila ports (López, 2014). These ports would act as trans-shipment ports for container shipping, and would also provide a transportation hub for Nicaraguan producers looking to access Atlantic markets. HKND have said that they will provide a Ports Operations Management Plan at a later date (HKND, 2014a: 77).

Critics have speculated about HKND and Wang's links to the Chinese Government. There is an argument that one does not get to be the twelfth richest man in China without having some connection to the Chinese Communist Party. The BBC's Carrie Gracie noted in her interview with Wang that 'He is happy to describe himself as a Chinese patriot' (Gracie, 2014). She also observed that Wang has hosted visits from communist party leaders at the headquarters of Xinwei in Beijing.

Despite Wang's denials, Xinwei certainly has links to the Chinese military. Santiago Villa's piece for Chamorro's *Confidencial* magazine makes great play of the fact that Xinwei has been working on an information system that will be 'the mind of the future Red Army'. Villa notes that Xinwei has tended to pursue 'government projects linked to the army, more than the large local market of private individuals' (Villa, 2014). Even if the project is, as Wang suggests, a private enterprise, it is certainly possible that it has the tacit approval of the government. Whether by design or not, HKND acts as a buffer which protects the government against the embarrassment of the project being delayed, subject to cost overruns or never being completed. This argument is advanced by Rebecca Keller who observes that the willingness of Chinese private investors to get involved in foreign direct investment initiatives such as this gives

'Beijing some protection against a risky investment' (Keller cited in Leach, 2014).

China and Latin America

HKND's involvement in Nicaragua is emblematic of the way in which Chinese companies and the Chinese state have intensified their engagement with Latin America in recent years. As investment in Latin America from US companies has decreased (by 20 per cent since 2011 according to a report on Channel News Asia), Chinese companies have moved in to fill the gap. While, as noted below, much of China's trade with Latin America has focused on primary commodities, infrastructure construction has also seen significant growth (Hill, 2014: 36), often fueled by the requirement for new transport facilities to ship the commodities. China has become the largest trading partner for a number of countries within the region.

Whereas in 2000 China's total trade with Latin America was in the region of $12 bn, by 2012 that figure had risen to approximately $250 bn. By 2014, loans from China's state-owned banks to Latin America exceeded the combined value of loans from the Inter-American Development Bank and the World Bank (BBC News, 2015). Chinese Premier Xi Jinping has promised to double China's trade with Latin America to a mammoth $500 bn over the next decade (Siow, 2015 online). R. Evan Ellis dates this new phase in Chinese-Latin American relations to 2009 when Chinese companies started to actually establish a physical presence in the region, marking a shift from China's long-standing policy of non-intervention. Ellis suggests that China has recognized that its economic well-being is at least partly dependent on the success of its commercial representatives abroad.

Driving trade between China and Latin America has been the former's need to secure reliable sources of metals, minerals, petroleum and foodstuffs. This in turn has driven Chinese investment in various infrastructure projects, of which the Nicaragua Canal is only one example. China is also funding a railway across Colombia and, news reports indicate, has signed an agreement with Brazil to build a railway between Brazil's Midwest and the Pacific Ocean. Chinese investment has fueled what has been a commodities boom in Latin America. Indeed, whilst much of the globe suffered from a dramatic economic slump in 2010, the demand for commodities meant that Latin America as a region was to some extent insulated from the worst effects of the slump. China has become Latin America's main customer. The Chinese have hoovered up everything from Venezuelan oil, to iron ore from Brazil, to copper from Peru (Ellis, 2014).

The picture is changing, however: commodities trade, investment, and prices have all dropped sharply in the past year as the delayed effects of the recession in China's main export markets have slowed the country's growth, and the Chinese Government has switched emphasis from overseas expansion to domestic consumption.

China and Taiwan

There is a further dimension to China's engagement with Central America in particular. Specifically, Central America is a key battleground in the diplomatic war between China and Taiwan. Francisco Haro Navejas argues that China's goal has been 'to corner Taiwan politically and diplomatically by portraying it as a rogue state' (Navejas, 2011: 205). Currently, there are only 23 countries that officially recognize Taiwan, and the number is diminishing. Beijing's 'one China' policy requires countries who wish to establish economic and trade relations with China to first end diplomatic relations with the government in Taipei.

Historically, Central America has been a region that has offered support to the Taiwanese in exchange for the promise of very significant investment. China's desire to offer support to the countries of the Isthmus is clearly driven in part by a wish to further isolate Taiwan and reduce further the number of countries that grant it official recognition (Peralta, 2010; Navejas, 2011). Navejas writes that China's 'ultimate goal is to displace Taiwan across the region' (Navejas, 2011: 205). Nicaragua actually ended its relation with Taiwan during the first Sandinista government. That decision was subsequently reversed after the Ortega government's electoral defeat in 1990 by Violeta Chamorro. Upon returning to power, Ortega did not end Nicaragua's ties to Taiwan and, in fact, 2006 saw Nicaragua sign a free trade agreement with the Taiwanese. While Nicaragua has not yet repudiated its relationship with Taiwan, there is no doubt that the Taiwanese government of Ma Ying-Jeou is uneasy about current developments.

The US and the Canal

While most observers believe that the Chinese Government must be behind the project in some way, it is in the interests of other countries and particularly the US to believe or pretend that this is not the case and that the project is indeed a private enterprise. As Jon Lee Anderson acknowledged: 'As long as the Canal is officially a private project, there is little benefit in provoking a public fight with China' (Anderson, 2014). The US and the Obama government have thus far remained curiously silent. No one invokes the Monroe Doctrine any more of course, but it is hard to believe that the US State Department is not concerned about the possibility of a strategically vital Canal, built and run by their principal global trade rival, taking shape in their own backyard. Some US-based critics have pointed to the fact that at 26 metres, the canal will be deep enough for Chinese submarines to be able to traverse it, and it is stretching credibility to believe that the Pentagon has not considered whose warships might transit the Canal if it is built, and what authority might determine such permissions.

The only comment on the Canal from an 'official' US source came in a statement released on 6 January 2015 by the embassy in Managua. This merely asked that various reports pertaining to the Canal's feasibility, financing and possible environmental impact be made available and indicated that the embassy was going to monitor the methodology for resolving property disputes. It would also be seeking clarification from the Nicaraguan Government on the bidding process for overseas companies. That is as far as the US government has gone. Perhaps mindful of the way in which any stronger American intervention would be viewed, Assistant Secretary of State for Western Hemisphere Affairs, Roberta Jacobson, confirmed to the *Tico Times* ahead of the Summit of the Americas held in Panama City in April 2014, that the US 'certainly doesn't necessarily plan to have a direct conversation with representatives of the Nicaraguan Government [about the Canal]' (cited in Luxner, 2015).

This 'wait and see' approach represents something of a change. During the Cold War, the US expended considerable energy and resources keeping communism out of its so-called 'backyard'. In one of the pivotal moments of the Cold War, the US engineered the over-throw of the left-leaning Guatemalan President Jacobo Arbenz in 1954 by supporting a coup instigated by Carlos Castillo Armas. In their efforts to quell the actions of 'guerrilla revolutionaries', Armas' forces received funding from the US government and training from US Special Forces. In El Salvador in the 1980s, the US supported the government in its savage repression of the civilian population. Right-wing paramilitary organizations such as ORDEN (*Organización Democrática Nacionalista*) deployed death squads to eliminate trade unionists and murdered thousands of workers and students who went on strike. Honduras, during the 1980s, was often referred to as 'the US' aircraft carrier' in Central America, home to huge US military bases within easy reach of trouble spots in neighbouring El Salvador, Guatemala and Nicaragua, and that military presence is still maintained today (Sanchez, 2014). In Nicaragua itself, the US financed, armed and trained the Contras in their fight against the Sandinistas after the latter's overthrow of the Somoza regime. The resulting scandal when it was discovered that the money for funding the Contras had come from the proceeds of arms sales to Iran – then under an arms embargo – was one of the defining moments of the Reagan Presidency and led to some uncomfortable questions about what Reagan actually knew.

Last, but not least, the US intervened constantly in Panama. Under the presidency of Theodore Roosevelt the US government in 1902 purchased the land and workings of the earlier, failed French canal attempt and paid $10 m to Panama in exchange for control of the Canal and its surrounding zone. As part of the deal the US supported the independence in 1903 of Panama from Colombia. The new canal opened in 1914. Until 1979 the Panama Canal Zone was a 'US governed region', effectively US territory. The canal company's directors were appointed by the US Secretary of the Army, and children born within the Zone were US citizens. Numerous US military bases were established in the Zone, most notably the HQ of the US Southern Command at Fort Clayton and the School of the Americas at Fort Gulick, which trained the military elites of most of the countries of Latin America. In 1977 President Jimmy Carter signed a treaty granting Panama full control of the Canal, so long as it would guarantee its permanent neutrality. This control was formally handed over on 31 December 1999 and the waterway was placed under the control of the Panama Canal Authority (ACP). Yet control and blatant intervention continued after 1977, most notably when the US invaded Panama in December 1989, deposed the country's dictatorial leader General Manuel Noriega and carted him off to be tried in US courts.

While such patterns of overt intervention might not be repeated in the twenty-first century in Nicaragua, it is inconceivable that the US will fail to consider with great care how it can exert influence and control over any strategic waterway that links the Atlantic and Pacific oceans.

The (Possible) Environmental Consequences of the Canal

Writing in *Revista Envío*, the head of the Nicaraguan Climate Change Alliance Víctor Campos Cubas labelled the Canal 'the greatest threat in history to the country's environmental conditions and the greatest risk of rendering the Nicaraguan population unable to meet its basic water and food security needs' (Campos, 2013). Meanwhile, writing in *Nature*, Nicaraguan microbiologist Jorge A. Huete-Pérez and German evolutionary biologist Axel Meyer warned that the project represents potential 'environmental disaster' for Nicaragua because it threatens 'some of the most fragile, pristine and scientifically important' areas within Central America (Huete-Pérez and Meyer cited in Clark Howard, 2014). The analyses and comments by these scientists are indicative of the horror with which the vast majority of environmentalists have responded to the prospect of the Canal. Organizations such as the Nicaragua Academy of Science and the Centro Alexander von Humboldt point to a whole raft of issues, including the threat of soil erosion, the increased risk of seismic activity, the risk of oil spills, habitat destruction and the threat of foreign organisms being introduced into the environment when ships crossing Lake Cocibolca dump ballast water.

Much of the focus has been on the possible effects on Lake Cocibolca, at 840,000 hectares the 19th largest lake in the world. All the proposed Canal routes involved the lake to a lesser or greater extent. Environmentalists have argued that the decision to take the Canal through the largest source of fresh water in Central America seems to run counter to the General

Water Law (Law 620) as well as to previous pronouncements made by Daniel Ortega. Law 620 states that the lake 'should be considered a natural reservoir for drinking water, as this is of the highest national interest and priority for national security'. In 2007, Ortega stated 'We can't risk [the] Lake (Cocibolca) for all the gold in the world. There won't be enough gold in the world to make us yield on this, because the Great Lake is Central America's greatest water reserve, and we're not going to put it at risk with a mega project like an interoceanic Canal' (*Revista Envío*, 2013a). Environmentalists claim that more frequent droughts caused by climate change will accentuate Lake Cocibolca's importance – especially since Nicaragua's population is growing.

The Nicaraguan Climate Change Alliance estimates that construction of the Canal will require the removal of some 832 million cubic metres of sediment from the bottom of the lake. While HKND believes that the amount of sediment stirred up by dredging can be minimized by using the very latest 'cut and suck' technology, environmentalists argue that it is inevitable that sediment will disperse throughout the lake once it is disturbed and that this will have a serious impact on water quality, particularly if the sediment is contaminated with pesticides and mercury (Zuidema, 2015). The lake already supplies drinking water to large populations (for example the city of Juigalpa) as well as irrigation water to farmers along the shores.

The dispersal of sediment could also have a serious impact on the lake's marine life. Lake Cocibolca is home to 40 native fish as well as 16 types of cichlids and a rare freshwater shark (Kraul, 2015). Sediment suspended in the water column could decrease the amount of light penetrating the water. That would kill the plants that sustain many of the lake's fish and would also promote the growth of algae. In the 'worst case scenario', according to Lindsey Fendt, Lake Cocibolca would become an 'aquatic dead zone' (Fendt, 2015b: 7). If that were to happen, notes Aran Son, 'there will be a segment of the population who will lose their livelihoods and have no skills – or land – for starting and/or maintaining another line of work' (Son, 2015).

It is not just marine life in Lake Cocibolca that would be threatened by the Canal; it would be wildlife throughout the region. The Canal will require the clearance of hundreds of thousands of hectares of jungle, dry forests, swamps and mangroves. Writing in *Nature*, Huete-Pérez and Meyer note in this context that 'The excavation of hundreds of kilometres from coast to coast will destroy around 400,000 hectares of rainforests and wetlands' (Huete-Pérez , 2014). The Centro Alexander von Humboldt Centre thinks that the Canal will threaten as many as a dozen endangered species (Watts, 2015), among them the green macaw, the spider monkey, the harpy eagle, Baird's tapir and the jaguar.

The Canal will also traverse parts of the Meso-American Biological Corridor, a system of reserves that stretch from Southern Mexico to Panama, which was established in the late 1990s with the support of Mexico, the seven countries of Central America and the World Bank to facilitate the migration of animals through the isthmus. The chosen route runs along the border of the Cerro Silva Nature Reserve and the Indo Maíz Biological Reserve, which together total some 673,000 hectares. The Canal would also run alongside the marshlands of the San Miguelito Wetlands, an area protected by the Ramsar Convention on Wetlands. At 520 metres wide, the Canal would, as Axel Meyer notes, constitute 'a huge barrier to gene flow and would clearly divide the American continent into two parts' (cited in Fendt, 2015b).

The problem was partially addressed in Panama by the construction of wildlife bridges and the Barro Colorado Island nature reserve which acts as a staging post for animals attempting to find a way across the Panama Canal (Fendt, 2015b: 8). According to Jonathan Watts, HKND's engineers have promised to build two bridges. Whether that will be sufficient, however, is highly debatable, (Watts, 2015).

The government, HKND and supporters of the Canal argue that it will benefit the environment. They contend that in shaving between 5,000 and 7,000 miles off the length of the journey from Asia to the Atlantic Ports, carbon emissions will be drastically reduced. The government and HKND argue that the Canal's ability to accommodate the largest ships, including the Triple-E ships of the Norwegian Maersk Line, will help to reduce the number of freight ships traversing the oceans.

Camilo Largo of the Nicaragua Recycling Forum contends that the Canal could indeed leave a very positive environmental legacy. He argues that the Canal's very viability is dependent on the government and HKND enacting a proactive environmental policy to ensure that the Canal has sufficient water with which to operate effectively. Supporters also argue that the doubling of GDP would, together with the government's policy of redistribution, lessen the likelihood of poor rural families migrating into protected areas such as the Indo Maíz Biological Reserve.

No one denies the validity of the concerns expressed by environmentalists, and government supporters claim that the Ortega administration and HKND are listening. HKND says that it has met with a number of environmental groups including the Wildlife Conservation Society, the Ramsar Convention, Fauna and Flora International, and the International Union for the Conservation of Nature, though it has not met with Nicaraguan environmental groups including the prestigious Centro Alexander von Humboldt. HKND has undertaken to offset any damage to the environment along the Canal's route by expanding wetland areas elsewhere. Moreover, the interim report on the project's environmental impact, produced by the respected London-based consultancy Environmental Resource Management (ERM), led HKND to make changes to its plans. The Canal will no longer cross the Sistema de Humedales de San Miguelito, and will instead run alongside it. The port at Brito on the Atlantic Coast has also been moved. The mangroves that form part of the Río Brito delta will be preserved by the building of a bridge, while the amount of salt water flowing into the river will be reduced through the construction of a concrete wall. Particularly significant is HKND's agreement to refrain from using explosives in the dredging of Lake Cocibolca. Finally, Wang's company has said that it will avoid any further intrusion into the Indo Maíz Biological Reserve.

Even if all other environmental objections can be met, Nicaragua's extreme volcanic susceptibility may yet defeat today's Canal project, as it did the earlier one in 1902. The recent eruption of the Telica Volcano (which is not on the Canal route) serves as a potent reminder of this vulnerability. Nicaragua has some 27 active volcanoes. Some of them are close to the Canal's proposed route. Ometepe Island, for example, which is situated in Lake Cocibolca itself, has two volcanoes – the largest of which, Concepción, has erupted two dozen times over the last 150 years (Huang and Billing, 2015). Its current status is 'restless'. Nor are volcanoes the only issue. Nicaragua is also subject to earthquakes. Indeed, there is a fault line running through Lake Cocibolca. In some ways, the issue of the Canal's susceptibility to seismic activity and natural disasters has been the 'elephant in the room', with few reports mentioning the issue, let alone giving it the attention it merits. It is worth bearing in mind the words of Panama's Foreign Minister, Fernando Núñez Fábrega, 'We didn't build the canal, the Americans built it. And the reason they eliminated Nicaragua is because there are earthquakes there. The second is because there are hurricanes there. And in Panama we don't have either' (Fábrega cited in *Revista Envío*, 2013b).

Through Indigenous Lands

Another source of controversy lies in the fact that the Canal passes through the Rama y Kriol territory, part of the Región Autónoma del Atlántico Sur (RAAS). Indeed, it is estimated that about 40 per cent of the Canal's route will pass through indigenous lands (Kilpatrick, 2015). The Rama y Kriol Territory, which covers close to 407,000 hectares, is home to several indigenous and Afro-descendant communities (Rama Cay, Monkey Point, Sumu Kaat, Tiktik Kaanu, Wiring Cay, Bangkukuk, Corn Rover, Indian Rover and Graytown) on the Miskito Coast – some 15,000 people in total. It is one of the poorest areas of Nicaragua. About half of the population is illiterate and some three-quarters live in poverty or extreme poverty (Kilpatrick, 2015). While the government points to the economic benefits that the Canal will provide for this impoverished region, many Rama worry about the effect of the Canal on their way of life and remain to be convinced of its benefits.

The Canal will likely bring a substantial number of outside workers, both Nicaraguan and foreign, into an area where the influx of outsiders – culturally Hispanic mestizo *colonos* from Pacific Nicaragua – has historically been a major source of contention. Mestizo colonization of the area accelerated in the 1990s after the war against the Contras had been resolved (Riverstone, 2006: 160). HKND is planning to build nine workers' camps along the canal's route, each capable of housing some 5,400 workers. While the company plans to establish 'designated hiring centres' in major regional towns and cities – Managua, Bluefields and Rivas for example – the risk of economic migrants moving into the Rama y

Kriol area looking for work remains. HKND has stated that the camps will be 'closed', with non-local workers barred from leaving unless as part of a company-organized outing. Moreover, the company is keen to avoid squatter camps and brothels springing up around these camps (HKND, 2014a: 38–40). However, it is doubtful whether the company can enforce this. Even the Head of the Canal Authority, Manuel Coronel Kautz, is sceptical. 'Where Nicaraguans work, everything happens', he told Tim Johnson, 'Prostitution will be rampant. I know that perfectly' (Johnson, 2015).

Many believe that the government's plans are illegal. As the President of Bangkukuk Carlos Wilson Bills stated in a documentary made by the Center for Assistance to Indigenous People:

> I feel like that big monster cannot just come and take us out of here. We have the last word about this issue of the Canal, because if we say we want it, they could come. But if we say we don't want it, it cannot come, because the land belongs to the Indian people. And we have the last word (cited in McGill, 2015).

Bills' comment speaks to indigenous sovereignty. Land rights have long been a major issue for the Rama and have brought them into conflict with various parties. Gerald Riverstone says that a powerful array of groups have been opposed to indigenous land rights, including local elites, national politicians and land speculators, as well as mestizo *colonos* (Riverstone, 2006: 154). The Canal is only the latest threat to the integrity of the Rama y Kriol territory. In 2007–08 the Rama people had denounced the arrival of several delegations at Monkey Point in their territory to assess the viability of constructing a deep-water port, railway (the so-called 'dry canal') and an oil pipeline (GTR-K, 2008). They have also had to deal with drug trafficking and with the sale of portions of their land on the internet (Riverstone, 2006: 160–162).

The rights of Nicaragua's indigenous communities are enshrined in the 1987 Constitution (and in its 1995 and 2000 reforms) in articles 5, 89 and 189. Moreover, the autonomy of these communities is guaranteed in Law 28 (*El Estatuto de Autonomía de las Regiones de la Costa Atlántica de Nicaragua*), while Law 445 (the 2003 *Ley del Régimen de Propiedad Comunal de los Pueblos Indígenas y Comunidades Étnicas de la Costa Caribe de Nicaragua y los Ríos Bocay, Coco, Indio y Maíz*) guarantees them property rights over the lands they inhabit (Kilpatrick, 2015). The latter was passed by the Nicaraguan Government after the Inter-American Court on Human Rights ruled against the government in the case *Mayangna Awas Tingni Community v. Nicaragua* (Riverstone, 2006: 172). The Canal's critics have pointed out that Law 445 demarcating indigenous territories in Nicaragua stipulates that this land cannot be sold or mortgaged or ceded to anyone. Nicaragua's Autonomy Statute further states that 'The communal lands are indissoluble; they cannot be donated, sold, leased, nor taxed, and they are eternal' (Article 36, point 1). Enshrined in Nicaraguan Law is the fact that the territorial government of the Rama y Kriol territory must also approve any use of the land.

The Rama y Kriol Territorial Government (GTR-K) issued guidelines that set out the terms and conditions under which they are prepared to consult with the government over the Canal. The *lineamientos* set out in the document were agreed by the Territorial Assembly in December 2014. These guidelines require the government in Managua to pay heed, first, to the various national and international conventions that protect the rights of Nicaragua's indigenous and Afro-descendant communities; second, to respect the rules and statutes that the GTR-K has passed and developed; and third, to consult in 'good faith'. Discussions must be based on 'full respect for its cultures, identities, customs and traditions, languages, social structures, histories and representative institutions' (GTR-K, 2014: 5). A range of further requirements is set out relating to transparency and inclusivity, and the guidelines put the onus squarely on the shoulders of the government to drive and pay for the consultation process.

While HKND has delivered a series of presentations to communities in affected areas, they admit that no formal consultations have taken place with indigenous communities, though there do appear to have been some moves to set something up. A letter addressed to the President of the Rama y Kriol Territorial Government, Héctor Thomas McCrea, from Hernán Estrada, Attorney General of the Republic, talks about establishing 'a process of dialogue and negotiation that allows us to define a perpetual rent for the use of the geographic area around the project' (Estrada, 2015). The letter, which appeared as part of an article on the Canal on the Al Jazeera America website, is dated 27 February 2015, two months after HKND broke ground, and appears to have been in response to the various legal actions brought by the Rama y Kriol Territorial Government against the government and HKND in regard to the Canal.

In August 2013, the Rama y Kriol territory government appealed to the Nicaraguan Supreme Court on the basis that Law 800 establishing the Grand Canal Authority had violated their rights. A year later in 2014, they announced that they were going to appeal to the Inter-American Commission on Human Rights on the grounds that the actions of the government and HKND had contravened the UN Declaration on the Rights of Indigenous Peoples (which Nicaragua signed in 2008) and the Organization of American States' Convention on Human Rights, as well as International Labour Organization Convention 169. In her presentation to the Inter-American Commission on Human Rights, the Rama's lawyer, Becky McCray, noted that 'The state's omission of material in consultation with Indigenous Peoples and Afro-descendants denies our relationship to our lands and our social structures, flagrantly violating our territorial rights, our right to participation, and our right to self-determination' (cited in McGill, 2015). The government has responded by asserting that the land is not being given away in perpetuity and is part of a concession that is limited – albeit one that could last for 100 years and could destroy the area in the meantime.

Clearly these reassurances are far from convincing. The planned deep water port at Punta Gorda, just to the south of Bangkukuk, one of the communities represented by the Rama y Kriol Territorial Government, will put at risk an entire way of life. For the government, this is very much a case of the needs of the country – of the many – outweighing the needs of the few. As in other disputes over indigenous land rights in Latin America, the problem from the government's perspective is that, as Anthony Stocks puts it, there is 'too much land for too few people' (Stocks, 2005: 97). The government and the Rama conceive of land differently. For the former, land is a commodity to be bought and sold. For the latter, however, it is much more than that. The Rama have an attachment to the land they inhabit which spans generations. Land in the Rama world view has ancestral links and spiritual-historical significance. For the Rama, Stocks notes, 'Land is often the home of spirits, not just the spirit owners. . . . Land holds a transcendental importance for indigenous identity', something that is 'difficult for people enculturated in the values of capitalist economies to appreciate' (Stocks, 2003: 345).

The Rama are fishermen, farmers and hunters who are dependent on the land for their livelihoods. The land provides food to eat and materials to construct their homes. According to Riverstone, the fact that they live in a 'multilocal residence pattern' whereby 'Rama families spend different months of the year in different parts of their territory' (Riverstone, 2006: 168) means that they 'require access to a large expanse of healthy coastal and forest ecosystems' (Riverstone, 2006: 154). The sense in which the Canal project has the potential to destroy the Rama's way of life is captured by Bangkukuk resident Edwin McCream in an interview with Al Jazeera America:

> It will destroy we. When I mean it will destroy we, we're not going to get turtle, we're not going to get fish, we're not going to get lobster, we're not going to get shrimp, and from the bush we're not going to get deer, we're not going to get gibnut [a type of rodent], we have no kind of animal if the Canal come (cited in Kilpatrick, 2015).

And it is not just the physical landscape of the Rama that will be affected. It is also their culture and heritage. While the residents of Bangkukuk speak the Kriol English that is characteristic of the Miskito Coast, some of the older residents continue to speak the nearly extinct Rama language, which is only spoken there. Efforts have been made to promote and preserve this language, which belongs to the Chibchan family of languages from Central America and Colombia, but many think that it will be destroyed by the forced relocation of the people of Bangkukuk. As McCray noted, 'If this project gets implemented, there is a strong possibility that the Rama language spoken in Bangkukuk Taik will disappear as the last people who speak that language get forcibly displaced from their land' (cited in McGill, 2015).

Protest along the Canal Route

While opinion polls have shown that most Nicaraguans are broadly in favour of the project, support does seem to have declined. A *Telesur* report from December 2014 noted that 'even centre-right opinion polls consistently indicate that over 70 per cent of people approve [of the Canal]' (Sefton, 2014). As Borge & Asociados noted: 'The announcement of the inter-oceanic canal has captured the imagination of the majority of the people' (Nicaragua News Bulletin, 2014). However a more recent poll undertaken by CID-Gallup in late May 2015 registered support for Ortega at 53 per cent (Johnson, 2015). Protests against the Canal have been particularly prominent along the Canal's route. Writing in the *Daily Telegraph*, Nina Lakhani observed that 'Along the planned route, [the Canal] is provoking a blend of anger, fear and defiance not witnessed since the Civil War ended' (Lakhani, 2014).

The project has generated protests and considerable ill feeling, some of which has exhibited a profound and sometimes openly racist anti-Chinese feeling. This is captured by environmental activist Franklin Briceño Martínez's observation that 'We are facing a new colonization by China. [. . .] We [. . .] don't want to become slaves of an Asian culture' (Johnson, 2015) and by placards waved by some demonstrators showing Chinese figures with grotesquely caricatured 'oriental' features. The resistance to HKND is part of a wider narrative and is a challenge faced by many Chinese companies working in Latin America and indeed elsewhere. Ellis points to several specific challenges: the fact that Chinese companies do not have much experience of working in

Latin America; 'a general distrust toward the Chinese'; workplace practices that don't sit well with Latin American workers; and a sense that Chinese companies are less concerned with environmental issues than they should be (Ellis, 2014).

In truth, the performance of Chinese companies in Latin America – particularly when it comes to preserving the environment – has been rather variable. As a recent report produced by Boston University indicates, the performance of Chinese investors within the region 'varies widely across different regulatory regimes and between more experienced and newer firms' (Ray et al., 2015: 3). Perhaps conscious of the need to boost the image of Chinese companies overseas and reassure those who have their doubts, the Chinese Government has instituted various safeguards designed to guide and regulate Chinese outbound investment. Chinese banks financing projects abroad are expected to adhere to the 'Green Credit Guidelines' that have been established by the China Banking Regulatory Commission (CBRC). This requires the banks to 'identify, assess, monitor, control and mitigate environmental and social risks' in any project that they might fund. In addition to the CBRC's 'Green Credit Guidelines', the Ministry of Commerce has also published the document 'Guidelines for Environmental Protection in Foreign Investment and Cooperation' and two of China's state-owned 'policy banks', the China Development Bank and the Export-Import Bank of China, have also adopted environmental safeguard strategies for projects that they finance (Ray et al., 2015: 14). However, as the Boston report notes, such measures can only be effective if they are enforced and if the dealings of Chinese companies in the region are transparent (Ray et al., 2015: 3). Clearly, the dealings of HKND have been anything but transparent.

The Canal project has also united small-holder indigenous farmers and ranchers in their resistance. Arnulfo Sequeira told the *Daily Telegraph* 'This is one of the most fertile regions in Nicaragua and the government have sold it behind our backs to the Chinese, they've sold our heritage, our sovereignty' (cited in Lakhani, 2014). Alba Lidia Espinoza from Obrejuelo (on Ometepe Island, Lake Cocibolca) noted, 'They've betrayed us. They betrayed our vote. They've sold the land and us like animals. We have nowhere to go. They've been selling us like slaves' (Membreño, 2014). A report in *Confidencial* from November 2014 reported that the government's approval of expropriation had already led to ten marches in as many municipalities through which the Canal will pass (Enríquez, 2014): 2 October in El Tule (Río San Juan), 3 October in San Jorge (Rivas), 8 October in La Unión (Nueva Guinea),10 October in Tola (Rivas), 15 October in San Miguelito (Río San Juan), 21 October in La Fonseca, 24 October in Moyogalpa (Isla de Ometepe), 28 October in Puerto Príncipe (RAAS), 1 November in Rivas, 20 November in Buenos Aires (Rivas), and 24 November in Potosí (Rivas) (Menbreño, 2014).

According to the Facebook page of *Nicaragua sin heridas*, there have been 46 protests against the Canal (as of 16 June 2015), the latest of which saw somewhere between 15,000 and 30,000 protestors (depending on the source) march in Juigalpa, capital of the Chontales department, which depends on Lake Cocibolca for its drinking water supply. These protests have seen demonstrators carrying barriers proclaiming 'The land is not for sale', 'Nicaragua will not give up!' and, most damagingly for Ortega, 'Ortega: vendepatria!' (Anderson, 2015). The phrase *vendepatria*, 'seller of our homeland', is pregnant with meaning. It was, as mentioned earlier, coined by Sandino himself, and it is also used a number of times by

Carlos Fonseca in *Viva Sandino*. Fonseca uses it to refer to President José María Moncada who, in making peace with the Americans (in contrast to Sandino) is accused of selling out the nation. He also uses it of the Conservatives who rebelled against the Liberals and the 'perfidia' oligarchs – the traditional families that dominated and controlled Nicaragua (Fonseca, 1974: 46–48).

Many are concerned about the prospect of having their property expropriated by the government. Those affected by the government's decision have formed the National Council for the Defence of our Lands, Lake and Sovereignty. HKND representatives have met with resistance whilst attempting to enter communities to conduct valuations of property, accompanied by armed police. Opponents of the Canal talk about the 'militarization' of the Canal route and of the communities along that route, an impression reinforced by the presence of soldiers and police. Opponents claim that this militarization has created an 'air of intimidation' which has served to 'stifle dissent' (Dyer, 2015). HKND estimates that some 29,000 people will be subject to compulsory purchase orders. However, other sources, including *The Daily Telegraph*, put the figure at closer to 100,000. A piece in Costa Rica's *Tico Times* by Larry Luxner claimed that the Canal could displace 'up to 119,000' (Luxner, 2015). Luxner further noted that the Canal could destroy some 2,800 private dwellings in three poorer municipalities, along with 96 schools, 19 health centres, and 90 churches (Luxner, 2015). While the government and Wang Jing have been at pains to assure those whose land will be expropriated that they will be fairly compensated, 'with no tricks or lies', many *campesinos* are sceptical. Critics have pointed out that valuations for expropriated land will be based on cadastral rather than market value. This means that compensation will be based on the value of land as set by the purchasers of the land for tax purposes which is almost always less than market value. Landowners can appeal against the value set by the government and HKND, but they have no right of appeal against the decision to expropriate their property.

Despite government denials, newspaper reports indicate that protests within the capital and along the route have been met with a heavy-handed response from the police and the authorities. A demonstration on a highway near El Tule in December 2014 saw police and protestors alike injured. Protestors claimed that the police used tear gas and rubber bullets to disperse them. The police claimed that protestors had attacked them with machetes, sticks and stones (Reuters, 2014). Protestors have also complained that the authorities and the police tried to stymie the protests by erecting barricades and harassing protestors as well as blocking mobile phone signals.

There have also been reports that foreign journalists have been harassed and ill-treated. A piece in the *Tico Times* from January 2015 pointed to the detention of journalists from both Belgium and Spain (Fendt, 2015a). More recently, Freedom House – admittedly a source likely to be hostile to the Ortega government – reported that Nicaragua had deported two activists belonging to the Center for Justice and International Law (CEJIL). One of them, Luis Carlos Buob, had been accused of drug trafficking by Nicaraguan immigration officials at the airport in Managua. Buob and his colleague Martha González were subsequently expelled. CEJIL activists had, along with activists from the Nicaraguan Center for Human Rights (CENIDH), protested to the Inter-American Human Rights Commission about possible abuses along the Canal's route (Freedom House,

2015). The expulsion of Buob and González has been condemned by several Nicaraguan groups, among them the Fundación Popul Na, the Autonomous Women's Movement and the National Council in Defence of Our Land, Lake and Sovereignty. Despite claims to the contrary from the government, such stories and episodes serve to fuel the suggestion that the authorities have little truck with potential dissenters.

Conclusion: Will the Canal ever happen?

For all the grandiosity and the ticker tape of the December 2014 ground-breaking ceremony, serious questions remain about the Canal. Given the vast scale of the project, there is considerable doubt that it can be completed in the five years scheduled by HKND and the Nicaraguan Government. The project has moved through its Pre-Construction Phase and is supposedly in the Early Works Construction Phase. This phase, which at least initially was slated to run until September 2015, should see the construction of access roads and the establishment of the infrastructure needed to build the Canal. Initially, the main Construction Phase was due to commence in September 2015 and finish in March 2020. However, recent news reports indicate that the main Construction Phase has been put back to March 2016 seemingly so that further work on the environmental impact of the Canal can be undertaken. The Construction Phase, whenever it takes place, will then be followed by a short Commissioning Phase (initially scheduled to run from April to June 2020) which will see the Canal segments filled with water and the locks tested (HKND, 2014.a: 53).

Meanwhile, news reports on the Canal's progress have slowed to a trickle. There was only a muted reaction to the news in early June 2015 that Environmental Resources Management had finally submitted its 14-volume report on the environmental and social impact of the Canal to the Nicaraguan Government. Initial reports were very light on detail. Telémaco Talavera told Nicaraguan state media that the ERM report 'says that the project offers potential benefits for the environment and the people of Nicaragua' (Castro, 2015). ERM spokesman

Manuel Román was quoted by Reuters as saying that the company had neither rejected nor endorsed the idea of the Canal. The report simply outlined the challenges facing HKND. It was for HKND and the government to work out solutions to those issues and problems.

ERM's website describes the company 'as a leading global provider of environmental, health, safety, risk, social consulting services and sustainability related services'. Certainly, the company enjoys an excellent reputation. Its work on the Nicaragua Canal, however, has attracted some criticism, particularly from environmentalists and scientists. Scientist Pedro Álvarez, for example, claimed that the company has 'been, at times, acting more like spokespersons for the project than independent assessors' (Lee, 2014). Reports on the ERM study have focused on the findings of a review panel invited by ERM to review 4 of the 14 chapters of the report in March 2015. The panel comprised 15 academics based mainly at universities in the United States. Their summary statement made a number of criticisms of ERM's work which were unsurprisingly seized upon by environmental NGOs opposed to the Canal project.

Among the weaknesses identified by the panel were the very short time period (about 18 months) set by HKND for completing the environmental study, and the 'inadequate resources' to undertake 'a proper sampling effort and analysis' (Nicaragua Canal Environmental Impact Assessment Review Panel, 2015: 1–2). The panel identified a number of specific concerns:

- the lack of knowledge of the make-up and composition of the sediments that will need to be dredged to facilitate the Canal;
- the fact that the hydrodynamic model which is used to predict the circulation of currents is based on a sample taken over the period of only a few days;

- 'the lack of sufficient data on water quality across Lake Nicaragua and inflowing rivers';
- the lack of data with which to judge 'post-construction water quality';
- an insufficient number of calibration points for the lake's geochemical modelling;
- a lack of attention to long-term climate forecasts which would provide a foundation for 'providing management alternatives' in response to climate change;
- concerns over the Canal's water balance;
- concerns over the artificial lake that will need to be built in the Rama y Kriol Territory to operate two sets of locks and which has the potential to disrupt native species as well as introduce invasive species;
- the seeming lack of planning to counteract the effects of deforestation;
- 'limited data on the use of habitats for foraging and spawning as well as seasonal migration of many species of fish' within the lake;
- a lack of data regarding the population viability of the various fish species inhabiting the lake;
- concerns that the lake will act as a 'physical barrier that inhibits animal movement and gene flow along the Meso-American Corridor';
- concerns that the Canal will have a negative impact on the endangered species which have been documented by the albeit 'cursory' terrestrial biodiversity surveys that have been undertaken;
- the lack of attention given to the importance of Nicaragua's Pacific coast for four species of sea turtles;
- the need for the review produced by ERM to incorporate and review relevant literature and reports pertaining to the lake and its inhabitants (Nicaragua Canal Environmental Impact Assessment Review Panel, 2015).

The concerns of the panel bear out the concerns expressed by environmentalists ever since the Canal project was announced and highlights the lack of thoroughness occasioned by the Government and HKND's excessive haste to have the project approved.

ERM responded by issuing a statement of its own which in many instances accepted the criticisms made by the review panel. ERM noted that the timescale for the report had been 'aggressive' and that they had recommended to the Government that several more studies be undertaken before a final decision is reached. Whilst the route of the canal is now seemingly set, ERM notes that the Government ought to look into further modifications to the plans that have been drawn up. Amongst the areas identified are the West Canal alignment, the design of the Camilo Lock and the location of the port on the Caribbean coast. In relation to sampling, ERM notes that while it does not disagree with the panel's concerns, the sampling methods undertaken were 'fit for purpose', and were based on Conservation International's Rapid Assessment Program. ERM states that it only reached conclusions on topics where it felt it had sufficient data and that it recommended to the government that further data be collected. Furthermore, ERM supports the panel's suggestions that climate change needs to be built into 'every aspect of the design'; that the effects of building the canal and plans for offsetting and mitigating those effects needs to be more clearly and substantially defined; and that an adequately funded management framework be established (ERM, 2015).

The government has clearly chosen its path. It has evidently decided that the potential economic benefits of the Canal outweigh any environmental negatives. It has also calculated that the environment can recover from the damage that the construction process will undoubtedly cause. For inspiration, the Nicaraguan Government surely looks south to Panama and to Panama City with its vibrant banking sector, skyscrapers and swish new apartment blocks. While inequality is a very significant problem in the 'Latin American Singapore', as in many Latin American countries (1 million people out of a population of 3.4 million are poor according to *The Economist* and the poorest 20 per cent of the population controls a mere 3.2 per cent of the country's wealth according to the World Bank), Panama still has the fastest growing economy in the region. Since 2004, according to *The Economist,* annual growth in GDP has never dropped below 7 per cent and, just before the world financial shock in 2007 reached 12.1 per cent. By contrast, Nicaragua's best figure in recent years was 5.7 per cent in 2011.

At the heart of Panama's prosperity is its Canal which, as Amalia Pérez notes, has 'injected astronomical amounts of capital into Panama's economy'. Pérez says that in the fiscal year 2014 alone, the Panama Canal generated some $1.9 bn in toll revenues (Perez, 2015), though the proceeds from the Canal are clearly not being shared throughout Panamanian society. As noted previously, the Panama Canal has undergone a significant expansion programme. This has provided a boost of 3.5 per cent to the country's GDP (*The Economist,* 2009).

Is the Nicaraguan Government right in its judgement that the economic benefits of the Canal outweigh any negative environmental impact? The government's economic rationale has been challenged by critics of the project. In a piece for *Revista Envío*, the economist Adolfo Acevedo Vogl argues that of the 50,000 jobs the government says will be created during the construction phase, only half will be for Nicaraguans. The remainder,

Annual GDP growth per cent		
Year	Panama	Nicaragua
2004	7.0+	
2005	7.0+	
2006	8.5	
2007	12.1	
2009	10.7	
2010	7.4	3.3
2011	10.8	5.7
2012	10.2	5.0
2013	8.4	4.6

Source: The Economist

Acevedo says, will be split between Chinese workers and workers from other countries. The promised 25,000 jobs represent just 0.6 per cent of the total annual employment projected for this period. Nor, according to Acevedo, will the construction of the Canal have the promised multiplier effect in terms of creating jobs in other sectors of the economy (Acevedo Vogl, 2015). Acevedo suggests that the initial construction phase will indeed see a significant influx of capital which will fuel an economic boom, one all the more acute because of the small size of the Nicaraguan economy. However, the quality of the jobs created by the boom will, he argues, be on the low side, with informal sectors receiving a particular boost. Moreover, the boost to the economy will be transitory. Once the construction phase concludes and the capital inflows coming into the country dry up, the boom period 'will be followed by the largest economic depression that has been registered in the history of Nicaragua and Central America'. The Canal, he concludes, will become 'a powerful, strictly private enclave under total and absolute control of the concessionary and its partners, separated for all intents and purposes from the rest of the country' (Acevedo Vogl, 2015).

Certainly, many questions remain about the Canal, relating to revenue streams, future administration and government and social effects. Will the canal generate sufficient income to repay the interest on the debts incurred in its construction? What will be the level of transit tolls and how will they compare with those of the Panama Canal? Who will operate the Canal once it is built – HKND on its own or in conjunction with the Nicaraguan Government? Who will administer the various sub-projects – the free trade zone, the ports and the tourist areas? What are the likely social effects of the Canal in terms of urbanization, migration and the risk of fuelling a sizeable black economy? The answers to these and other questions will only become apparent as the canal project develops and the building work really starts to gather momentum – assuming, of course, that it does.

Given the issues at stake, particularly the expropriation of land, and the potentially volatile mix of former Contras and former Sandinistas among those most affected, particularly on the Atlantic Coast, it is possible that as the Canal project progresses and takes shape, things could turn nasty. The government is calculating that resistance will dissipate once the anticipated economic benefits start to filter through to the population. However, the tone of some of the rhetoric emanating from the farming and indigenous communities along the Canal's path suggests that the government will face a difficult task removing them. There is a risk that compulsory evictions will turn violent, with some communities threatening to take up arms to protect their homes. The threat is not an empty one: armed conflict has broken out before between indigenous communities and mestizo *colonos,* and land has always been and remains a key source of conflict between Nicaragua's coastal people and the Sandinista government. Many of these communities have a very real attachment to the land they inhabit. The Canal project can be folded into a wider history of the struggle for autonomy and *costeño* identity. Whatever the government and HKND might think, it is very difficult to put a price on land that is ancestral or has been held for many generations.

Whilst the present consensus outside the country is that the Canal will never be completed, some have said that Nicaragua could still be left with a significant consolation prize. Isabel López writes that 'The promise of the sub-projects encourages the expectations of some local businesses that doubt the viability of the Canal, but wager that this adventure could leave the country with a consolation prize, some roads, a port, and perhaps as much as a big tourist project' (López, 2014). Of course, there is also the possibility that HKND and Ortega will pull this off. For all his failings, Ortega is no fool. He has mortgaged his political future and his legacy on the Nicaraguan Canal. He surely would not have done so had he not been confident of success.

References

Acevedo Vogl, A. (2015) 'El Gran Canal y las "grandes" expectativas de empleo' *Revista Envío* [online] Número 394 Febrero. <http://www.envio.org.ni/articulo/4964> [Accessed 2 March 2015].

Alpieldelapalabra (2014) 'Eduardo Galeano: Canal de Nicaragua' *Alpieldelapalabra* [online] 30 Noviembre. <http://alpialdelapalabra.blogspot.co.uk/2014/11/eduardo-galeno-canal-de-nicaragua.html> [accessed 5 January 2015].

Anderson, J. L. (2015) 'Breaking Ground on the Nicaragua Canal', *The New Yorker* [online] 2 January. <http://www.newyorker.com/news/news-desk/breaking-ground-nicaragua-Canal> [Accessed 5 January 2015].

Anderson, J.L. (2014) 'The Comandante's Canal', *The New Yorker* [online] 10 March. <http://www.newyorker.com/magazine/2014/03/10/the-comandantes-Canal> [Accessed 20 December 2014].

Arsenault, C. (2011) 'Nicaragua's Ortega: Socialism to opportunism?' *Al Jazeera* [online] 8 November. <http://www.aljazeera.com/indepth/features/2011/11/2011117173951437487.html> [Accessed 21 April 2015].

Baracco, L. (2005) *Nicaragua: The Imagining of a Nation*, New York: Algora Publishing.

BBC News (2015) 'Venezuela "receives $5bn in finance from China"' *BBC News* [online] 20 April. <http://www.bbc.co.uk/news/world-latin-america-32381250> [Accessed 21 April 2015].

Caistor, N. (2009) 'Re-election issue divides Nicaragua', *BBC News* [online] 20 October. <http://news.bbc.co.uk/1/hi/8316445.stm> [Accessed 24 August 2015].

Campos Cubas, V.M. (2013) 'The Canal will irreversibly damage Lake Cocibolca', *Revista Envio* 384 [online]. <www.envio.org.ni/articulo/4726> [Accessed 24 August 2015].

Castro, I. (2015) 'Nicaragua Canal project study delivered, details scarce' *Reuters* [online] 1 June. <http://www.reuters.com/article/2015/06/01/nicaragua-Canal-idUSL1N0YN1T020150601> [Accessed 1 June 2015].

Chamorro, C.F. (2014) 'Ortega, Wang Jing y el Canal por Nicaragua' *El País* [website] 23 Julio. <http://internacional.elpais.com/internacional/2014/07/23/actualidad/1406131911_536133.html> [Accessed 11 May 2015].

Clark, H.B. (2014) 'Nicaraguan Canal Could Wreck Environment, Scientists Say' *National Geographic* [online] 22 February. <http://news.nationalgeographic.com/news/2014/02/140220-nicaraguan-canal-environment-conservation/> [Accessed 24 August 2015].

Clayton, L. (1987) 'The Nicaragua Canal in the Nineteenth Century: Prelude to American Empire in the Caribbean' *Journal of Latin American Studies* 19:2 323–352.

Dyer, Z. (2015) 'Nicaragua Canal project surrounded by air of intimidation, opponents say' *Tico Times* [online] 10 June. <http://www.ticotimes.net/2015/06/10/nicaragua-Canal-project-surrounded-air-intimidation-opponents-say> [Accessed 10 June 2015]

Ellis, R.E. (2014) *China on the Ground in Latin America: Challenges for the Chinese and Impacts on the Region* London: Palgrave Macmillan.

Enríquez, O. (2014) 'La "teleraña" de Wang Jing' in O. Enríquez, S. Villa, W. Miranda (eds.) *La "teleraña" de Wang Jing y la conexión militar con China,* on *Confidencial* [online], <http://www.confidencial.com.ni/la-telarana-de-wang-jing> [Accessed 11 May 2015].

Envío Team (2013a) 'The challenge of the others' *Revista Envío* [online] Number 384 Julio. <http://www.envio.org.ni/articulo/4724> [Accessed 24 August 2015].

Envío Team (2013b) 'Notes written beneath the trees of life' *Revista Envío* [online] Number 385 Agosto. <http://www.envio.org.ni/articulo/4733> [Accessed 24 August 2015].

Envío Team (2014) 'Will we always use violence to deal with our problems?' *Revista Envío* [online] Number 397 Agosto. <http://www.envio.org.ni/articulo/4893> [Accessed 24 August 2015].

ERM (2015) 'ERM Response to Summary Statement of Nicaragua Canal Environmental Impact Assessment Review Panel' *Circle of Blue* [online] 5 June. <http://www.circleofblue.org/waternews/wp-content/uploads/2015/06/ERM-respnse-to-Nicaragua-Canal-International-Expert-Panel-Comment-Response_Master-5.13.2015_English.pdf>[Accessed 24 August 2015].

Estrada, H. (2015) 'Letter to Héctor Thomas McCrea' [online] 27 February. <https://www.documentcloud.org/documents/1794660-letter-small.html>

Fendt, L. (2015a) 'Journalists harassed, detained in latest chapter of Nicaragua Canal saga', *Tico Times* [online] 7 January.
<http://www.ticotimes.net/2015/01/07/journalists-harassed-detained-in-latest-chapter-of-nicaragua-canal-saga> [Accessed 24 August 2015].

Fendt, L. (2015b) 'Canal project still a puzzle after formal start' *EcoAméricas* [website] 17:4 6–8 February. <http://www.ecoamericas.com/en-US/issue.aspx?id=196> [Accessed 2 April 2015].

Freedom House (2015) 'Nicaragua Expels Critics of Canal Project' *Freedom House* [online] 18 May. <https://freedomhouse.org/article/nicaragua-expels-critics-Canal-project#.VVsc-PldX6c> [Accessed 1 June 2015].

Fonseca, C. (1974) *Viva Sandino Memorias de la Lucha Sandinista* [website], <https://memoriasdelaluchasandinista.org/media/textos/98.textos.pdf> [Accessed on 16 June 2015].

Fonseca, C. (1969) *Nicaragua Hora Cero* Managua: Secretaría Nacional de Propaganda y Educación Política de FSLN. *Centro de Documentación de los Movimientos Armados* [online]. <http://www.cedema.org/ver.php?id=2494> [Accessed 24 August 2015].

Global Consilium (2015) 'The Nicaragua Canal: A dream come true?' *Global Consilium* [online] 29 January. <http://globalconsilium.com/2015/01/29/the-nicaragua-Canal-a-dream-come-true/> [Accessed 19 March 2015].

Gobierno Territorial Rama y Kriol (GTR-K) (2008) *Comunicado de Prensa* signed by Pearl Marie Watson, First Secretary, GTR-K

Gobierno Territorial Rama y Kriol (GTR-K) (2015) 'Lineamientos para realizar un proceso de consulta en el territorio Rama y Kriol en relación al Proyecto del Gran Canal Interoceánico de Nicaragua y sub-proyectos asociados' [online]. <https://s3.amazonaws.com/s3.documentcloud.org/documents/1794626/lineamientos-watermark.pdf> [Accessed 15 June 2015].

Gracie, C. (2015) 'Wang Jing: The man behind the Nicaragua Canal project', *BBC News* [online] 18 March. <http://www.bbc.co.uk/news/world-asia-china-31936549> [Accessed 19 March 2015].

Grant, U. (1881) 'The Nicaraguan Canal' *North American Review* 132.

Hamilton, J. (2008) 'Shallow water ahead for Panama Canal', *NPR* online] 3 March. <http://www.npr.org/templates/story/story.php?storyId=87851345> [Accessed 31 July 2015].

Háskel, G. (2014) 'Nicaragua Canal project seen having geopolitical, not just trade implications' *Buenos Aires Herald* [online] 21 July. <http://buenosairesherald.com/article/165077/nicaragua-Canal-project-seen-having-geopolitical-not-just-trade-implications> [Accessed 16 February 2015].

HKND (2014a) *Nicaragua Canal Project Description* [online] December 2014. <http://hknd-group.com/upload/pdf/20150105/Nicaragua_Canal_Project_Description_EN.pdf> [Accessed 6 July 2015].

HKND (2014b) Company News: *Commencement of Nicaragua Interoceanic Canal* [online] December 2014.

<http://hknd-group.com/portal.php?mod=view&aid=145> [Accessed 24 August 2015].

Hill, D. (2014) 'China and Latin America: Which way now?' *China Dialogue, China overseas: looking beyond the headlines* London and Beijing: China Dialogue 31–35. <https://www.chinadialogue.net/reports/7432-China-overseas-looking-beyond-the-headlines/en> [Accessed 2 May 2015].

Huang, L. & Billing, C. (2015) 'Mystery Surrounds Chinese Investment in Nicaraguan Canal Project' *Radio Free Asia* [online] 26 May. <http://www.rfa.org/english/news/china/mystery-surrounds-chinese-investment-in-nicaraguan-canal-project-05262015143309.html> [Accessed 27 May 2015].

Huete-Pérez, J.A. & Meyer, A. (2013) 'Conservation: Nicaragua Canal could wreak environmental ruin' *Nature* [online] 506.7488 19 February 2014. <http://www.nature.com/news/conservation-nicaragua-canal-could-wreak-environmental-ruin-1.14721> [Accessed 24 August 2015].

Jinping, X. (2013) 'Xi in call for building of new "maritime silk road"' *China Daily USA* [online] 4 October. <http://usa.chinadaily.com.cn/china/2013-10/04/content_17008940.htm> [Accessed 28 August 2015]

Johnson, T. (2015) 'Will China finally fulfil Nicaragua's dream of an inter-ocean canal?' *Miami Herald* [online] 18 June. <http://media.mcclatchydc.com/static/features/NicaCanal/> [Accessed 6 July 2015].

Kilpatrick, K. (2015) 'Canal "Will Destroy We"' *Al Jazeera America* [online] 19 April. <http://projects.aljazeera.com/2015/04/nicaragua-Canal/displaced.html> [Accessed 24 August 2015].

Kinzer, S. (2015) 'Daniel Ortega is a Sandinista in name only' *Al Jazeera America* [online] 6 April. <http://america.aljazeera.com/opinions/2015/4/daniel-ortega-is-a-sandinista-in-name-only.html> [Accessed 27 April 2015].

Lakhani, N. (2014) 'Giant Canal threatens way of life on the banks of Lake Nicaragua', *The Telegraph*

[online] 26 October. <http://www.telegraph.co.uk/
news/worldnews/centralamericaandthecaribbean/
nicaragua/11167697/Giant-Canal-threatens-way-of-
life-on-the-banks-of-Lake-Nicaragua.html> [Accessed 1
November 2014].

Leach, P.T. (2015) 'Are Nicaragua Canal plans driven by
geopolitics?' *Journal of Commerce* [online]. <http://
www.joc.com/maritime-news/trade-lanes/are-
nicaragua-Canal-plans-driven-geopolitics_20141020.
html> [Accessed 27 April 2015].

Lee, B. (2014) 'Nicaragua's Canal Project Pushes Forward
Despite Economic, Environmental Questions'
International Business Times [online] 15 August.
<http://www.ibtimes.com/nicaraguas-canal-project-
pushes-forward-despite-economic-environmental-
questions-1655176> [Accessed 6 July 2015].

López, I. (2014) 'La lotería de sub-proyectos' in O.
Enríquez , S. Villa, W. Miranda (eds.) *La "teleraña"
de Wang Jing y la conexión militar con China* in *Confidencial* [online]. <http://www.confidencial.com.ni/
la-telarana-de-wang-jing> [Accessed 11 May 2015].

Luxner, L. (2015) 'Activists visiting Washington blast
Nicaragua's $50 billion Canal project as "illegiti-
mate"', *Tico Times* [website] 6 April. <http://www.
ticotimes.net/2015/04/06/activists-visiting-washington-
blast-nicaraguas-50-billion-Canal-project-as-illegitimate>
[Accessed 27 April 2015].

McGill, M. (2015) 'Construction of Nicaragua Canal
Threatens Indigenous Lives and Livelihoods' *Cultural
Survival* [online] 19 May. <http://www.culturalsurvival.
org/news/construction-nicaragua-Canal-threatens-
indigenous-lives-and-livelihoods> [Accessed 21 May
2015].

Maes, J.M. (2014) 'The Canal will affect ecosystems,
species and even genes' *Revista Envío* [online]
Number 398 September. <http://www.envio.org.ni/
articulo/4904> [Accessed 24 August 2015].

Malsin, J. (2015) 'Egypt hails $8bn Suez canal expansion as
gift to world at lavish ceremony', *The Guardian* [online]

6 August 2015. <http://www.theguardian.com/world/2015/aug/06/egypt-suez-canal-expansion> [Accessed 7 August 2015].

Membreño, C. (2014) '"¡Qué se vayan los chinos"' in O. Enríquez, S. Villa, W. Miranda (eds.) *La "telaraña" de Wang Jing y la conexión militar con China* in *Confidencial* [online]. <http://www.confidencial.com.ni/la-telerana-de-wang-jing> [Accessed 11 May 2015].

Navejas, F.H. (2011) 'China's Relations with Central America and the Caribbean States: Reshaping the Region' in A. Hearn and J.L. León-Manríquez (eds.) *China Engages Latin America: Tracing the Trajectory* Boulder Col: Lynne Rienner Publishers 203–219.

Nicaragua Canal Environmental Impact Assessment Review Panel (2015) 'Summary Statement' *Circle of Blue* [online] 5 June. <http://www.circleofblue.org/waternews/wp-content/uploads/2015/06/Nicaragau-FIU-Panel-Summary.13-April-2015-Final.pdf> [Accessed 15 June 2016].

Nicaragua News Bulletin (2014) 'New polls reveal views on Canal, economic situation of Nicaraguans' *NicaNet* [online] 14 October, <http://www.nicanet.org/?page=blog&id=30325> [Accessed 2 November 2015].

Nicaragua Solidarity Campaign (2014) 'Nicaragua's interoceanic Canal: will the benefits outweigh the risks?' *Nicaragua Solidarity Campaign* [online] July. <http://www.nicaraguasc.org.uk/resources/Briefing-Interoceanic-Canal-July-2014.pdf>[Accessed 2 November 2014].

Oquist, P. (2015) 'The Grand Interoceanic Canal in the Economic Development of Nicaragua, Central America and Latin America' private talk delivered at Canning House, London, 17 June, reported [online] at: <http://www.el19digital.com/articulos/ver/titulo:30565-ministro-paul-oquist-promueveinversiones-en-londres>

Peralta, G.A. (2010) 'Central America between Two Dragons: Relations with the Two Chinas' in A.E.

Fernández Jilberto and B. Hogenboom (eds.) *Latin America Facing China: South-South Relations beyond the Washington Consensus*, pp. 167–179, New York and Oxford: Berghahn Books.

Pérez, A. (2015) 'Nicaragua is Not For Sale: The Culmination of President Ortega's Inconsistent Presidency' *Council on Hemispheric Affairs* [online] 8 July. <http://www.coha.org/nicaragua-is-not-for-sale-the-culmination-of-president-ortegas-inconsistent-presidency/> [Accessed 14 July 2015].

Ray, R., Gallagher, K.P., Lopez, A. & Sanborn, C. (2015) *China in Latin America: Lessons for South-South Cooperation and Sustainable Development* Boston University, Centro de Investigación para la Transformación, Tufts University, Universidad del Pacífico [online]. <http://www.bu.edu/pardeeschool/files/2015/04/Working-Group-Final-Report-Pages1.pdf> [Accessed 1 June 2015].

Reuters (2014) 'At least 21 injured in protest against Nicaragua Canal: police' *Reuters* [online] 24 December. <http://www.reuters.com/article/2014/12/24/us-nicaragua-Canal-idUSKBN0K21AR20141224> [Accessed 27 December 2014].

Riverstone, G. (2006) 'The Political Ecology of Indigenous Land Tenure' in M. González et al. (eds.) *El Pueblo Rama Luchando por Tierra y Cultura / The Rama People Struggling for Land and Culture* Managua: URACCAN / University of Tromsö Press 153–179.

Rogers, T. (2011) 'President Daniel Ortega Isn't a Nice Guy, but Nicaraguans Will Re-elect Him Anyway' *Time* [online] 4 November. <http://content.time.com/time/world/article/0,8599,2098720,00.html> [Accessed 2 November 2014].

Sánchez, A. (2014) 'Honduras becomes US military foothold for Central America' *NACLA* [online]. <https://nacla.org/news/honduras-becomes-us-military-foothold-central-america> [Accessed 1 August 2015].

Sandino, A.C. (1929) [2014] 'Plan de realización del supremo sueño de Bolívar' in G.M. Martínez (ed.)

Historia de la Defensa por la Soberanía, Nacional contada por el General Augusto C. Sandino Managua: Alcaldía de Managua La Alcaldía del Poder Ciudadano. <http://www.managua.gob.ni/modulos/documentos/revista/SANDINO2014.pdf> [Accessed 16 June 2015].

Sefton, S. (2014) 'Who's afraid of the Nicaraguan Canal' *TeleSur* [online] 14 December. <http://www.telesurtv.net/english/analysis/Whos-Afraid-of-the-Nicaraguan-Canal-20141210-0046.html> [Accessed 27 December 2014].

Siow, M. (2015) 'China-Latin America ties raise concerns' *Channel NewsAsia* [online] 19 April. <http://www.channelnewsasia.com/news/business/china-latin-america-ties/1793010.html> [Accessed 27 April 2015].

Small, G. (2015) 'The Maritime Silk Road Comes to the Americas' *Executive Intelligence Review* 42: 2 [online] 9 January. <http://www.larouchepub.com/other/2015/4202canal_nicaragua_silk_rd.html> [Accessed 24 August 2015].

Smith, R. (2014) 'Is Nicaraguan Canal a Boon for Trade or a Boondoggle?' *National Geographic* [online] 29 March. <http://news.nationalgeographic.com/news/2014/03/140329-nicaragua-canal-hknd-panama-wang-jin-world/> [Accessed 14 April 2014].

Son, A. (2015) 'Realistic US Foreign Policy Options for Nicaragua', *International Policy Digest* [online] 22 February. <http://www.internationalpolicydigest.org/2015/02/22/realistic-u-s-foreign-policy-options-for-nicaragua/> [Accessed 6 July 2015].

Stocks, A. (2005) 'Too Much for Too Few: Problems of Indigenous Land Rights in Latin America' *Annual Review of Anthropology* 34: 85–104.

Stocks, A. (2003) 'Mapping Dreams in Nicaragua's Bosawas Reserve' *Human Organization* 62: 344–356.

The Economist (2008) 'A plan to unlock prosperity' *The Economist* [online] 3 December. <http://www.economist.com/node/15014282> [Accessed 4 June 2015].

Villa, S. (2014) 'Wang, Xinwei, y la "conexión military"' in O. Enríquez, S. Villa, W. Miranda (eds.) *La "teleraña" de Wang Jing y la conexión militar con China* on *Confidencial* <http://www.confidencial.com.ni/la-telarana-de-wang-jing> [Accessed 11 May 2015].

Walker, T.W. and Wade C.J. (2011) *Nicaragua Living in the Shadow of the Eagle*, Boulder Colorado: Westview Press.

Watts, J. (2015) 'Land of opportunity – and fear – along route of Nicaragua's giant new Canal' *The Guardian* [online] 20 January. <http://www.theguardian.com/world/2015/jan/20/-sp-nicaragua-canal-land-opportunity-fear-route> [Accessed 20 January 2015].

White, R. (2015) 'Nicaragua's Grand Canal: 1 – Schism amongst the Sandinistas' *Latin America Bureau* [online] 12 January. <http://lab.org.uk/nicaraguas-gran-Canal-1-schism-amongst-the-sandinistas> [Accessed 12 January 2015].

White, R. (2015) 'Nicaragua's Grand Canal: 2 – The environment vs the economy', *Latin America Bureau* [online] 14 January. <http://lab.org.uk/nicaraguas-grand-Canal-2-the-environment-vs-the-economy> [Accessed 14 January 2015].

White, R. (2015) 'Nicaragua's Grand Canal: 3 – No excavation without consultation', *Latin America Bureau* [online] 20 January. <http://lab.org.uk/nicaraguas-grand-Canal-3-no-excavation-without-consultation> [Accessed 20 January 2015].

White, R. (2015) 'Nicaragua's Grand Canal: 4 – The Emperor's New Funds' *Latin America Bureau* [website] 29 January. <http://lab.org.uk/nicaraguas-grand-Canal-4-the-emperors-new-funds> [Accessed 29 January 29 2015].

White, R. (2015) 'Nicaragua's Grand Canal: 5 – The Geopolitics of the Canal' *Latin America Bureau* [online] 2 March. <http://lab.org.uk/nicaraguas-grand-Canal-5-the-geopolitics-of-the-Canal> [Accessed 2 March 2015].

Whitefield, M. (2015) 'Water begins to fill massive Panama Canal Expansion Locks' *Miami Herald* [online] 28 June.<http://www.miamiherald.com/news/nation-world/world/americas/article25717330.html> [Accessed 31 July 2015].

Zuidema, T. (2015) 'Will the Nicaragua Canal ruin the "Galapagos of Central America"' *Tico Times* [online] 26 January. <http://www.ticotimes.net/2015/01/26/will-the-nicaragua-Canal-ruin-the-galapagos-of-central-america> [Accessed 27 April 2015].

Lightning Source UK Ltd.
Milton Keynes UK
UKOW06f0837020616

275453UK00008B/96/P